C000046668

ANOREXIA & BULIMIA

Control That Is Out of Control

JUNE HUNT

ROSE PUBLISHING/ASPIRE PRESS

Torrance, California

ROSE PUBLISHING/ASPIRE PRESS

Anorexia & Bulimia: Control That Is Out of Control
Copyright © 2014 Hope For The Heart
All rights reserved.
Aspire Press, a division of Rose Publishing, Inc.
4733 Torrance Blvd., #259
Torrance, California 90503 USA
www.aspirepress.com

Register your book at www.aspirepress.com/register
Get inspiration via email, sign up at www.aspirepress.com

For more information on Hope For The Heart, visit www.hopefortheheart.org or call 1-800-488-HOPE (4673).

Printed by Regent Publishing Services Ltd.
Printed in China, February 2015, 2nd printing

CONTENTS

𝒟ear friend,

It was a Friday evening and I had just finished speaking before an audience of 600 when a distraught woman came forward baring her soul, overwrought with emotion.

"My daughter died of anorexia," Brenda (not her real name) sobbed. "She was just 22 and meant the world to me. She was so vibrant, so precious. Then she withered away to nothing."

As she spoke the word "nothing," Brenda's body wilted, then she began to wail. At that moment, I felt the heartbreak of a desperate mother watching her own daughter shrinking down to "skin and bones," dying of self-imposed starvation. This endeared daughter was unable to recognize her own distorted thoughts: thinking she was much too fat, when instead she was much too thin, thinking she was eating too much, when instead she was eating too little. She was slowly starving herself to death.

In the months that followed, Brenda was consumed with bitterness ...

▶ *At her husband* for not taking the problem seriously.

- "She's just going through a phase."

▶ *At her friends* for not giving compassion, just trivialities.

- "She's so cute and trim and doesn't want to be fat!"

- ▶ *At family members* for not understanding the real issues.
  - "Just *make* her eat!"

- ▶ *At the doctors* for not being more proactive.
  - "Don't worry. We're watching her."

- ▶ *At the hospital* for not supplying life-saving solutions.
  - "We're doing all we can."

- ▶ *At herself* for not knowing what to do—sooner.
  - "I've never been here before!"

- ▶ *At God* for not rescuing her precious child.
  - "Why didn't *He* make her eat?"

- ▶ *At her daughter* for not fighting to live (until the last three months)[1]
  - "Why would she choose to leave me—to wither away and die?"

Brenda's heartrending story helps explain why real solutions—*effective* solutions—must be offered to those searching for help and hope. Practical answers must address this problem on multiple fronts. In reality, strugglers and their families need help with all aspects of eating disorders—the mental, medical, and emotional dimensions, as well as the social and spiritual.

Most people don't understand eating disorders at all. For example, *anorexia* and *bulimia* appear to be opposites: the anorexic stops eating, while the bulimic keeps overeating—but neither condition has much to do with food. Instead, both strugglers are starving—for unconditional love, significance, and security.

Both feel they don't have control of their lives, so they substitute the one area they *can* control—their *weight*. They can control what they put into their mouths and how long they keep it there. This daily destructive cycle explains why I refer to eating disorders as "control that is out of control!"

In our media-saturated culture, where "thin is in," where people *go all out* for perfect appearance, we need to know, *"The Lord doesn't see things the way you see them. People judge by outward appearance, but the Lord looks at the heart"* (1 Samuel 16:7).

How vital that we see ourselves from God's point of view. Ultimately, when you allow God's truth about you to take control of your thoughts, your actions will change, and then your life will change. Jesus says it this way, *"The truth will set you free"* (John 8:32).

Over the years, I have personally counseled hundreds of people who have found lasting freedom. My prayer is that this small book—filled with biblical hope and practical help—will bless you on your journey and then help you be a guide and blessing to others.

Yours in the Lord's hope,

June

June Hunt

ANOREXIA & BULIMIA
Control That Is Out of Control

"I miss Ana," she laments.[2] Her dear friend is gone. And with that departure, her world turned upside down.

But now she wants everything back to the way it used to be. That's when she had control over her life. That's when Ana was crucial in her life. Yet others objected—those who forced Ana away.

Today, however, she has asked Ana to return, and she's determined to get Ana back—her familiar friend, her best friend, her only friend called Ana— short for Anorexia.

It's startling! Around the globe, growing numbers characterize themselves as "pro-ana," namely, *pro-anorexic* or prone to self-starvation. They wear the label with pride, attaching it to their slowly withering figures. They claim, "Anorexia is not an eating disorder but rather a *lifestyle choice.*" And now hundreds of "pro-ana" websites dispense their dark, distorted message of death.

Websites and blogs alike help them link forces internationally to share tragic tips on everything from *how to become anorexic* to *how to hide their non-eating habits.* And for the "Mias" (short for *Bulimia*), who binge and purge food, there are "pro-mia" sites as well.

An unmistakable cloud of darkness hovers over these deadly eating disorders. Meanwhile, too many *Anas* and *Mias* in the world proudly declare that they're simply *dying to be thin*.[3]

For those who are painfully deluded, God's plan is dramatically different from the one destroying their lives. For today, God wants them to eat and enjoy the daily bread He provides, and He wants to be their *"bread of life"* for all their tomorrows.

For it was Jesus who said ...

"I am the bread of life."
(John 6:48)

DEFINITIONS

Karen Carpenter—the internationally acclaimed vocalist—could never have imagined being "center stage" for anything other than her music.

She was the sister in the sibling duo *The Carpenters*—a sound sensation in the 1970s and early 80s that repeatedly rose to the top of the pop music charts. Songs like "We've Only Just Begun" and "Close to You" contributed to this Grammy award-winning pair's achieving worldwide sales of albums and singles exceeding 100 million.[4] Karen was known for her vibrant glow and velvety voice, a combination that ignited invitations for stage performances all around the world.

But February 4, 1983, marked her final curtain call. Found unconscious at her parents' home, she was rushed to the hospital, where shortly after she was pronounced dead. Karen died of a heart attack at the tender age of 32, but it was her medical diagnosis that once again catapulted her back on "center stage."

Proverbs, the biblical book of wisdom, presents this painful truth ...

> **"There is a way that seems right ...**
> **but its end is the way to death."**
> **(Proverbs 16:25 ESV)**

Before Karen Carpenter's death, the word *anorexia*—unknown to the average person—was only occasionally uttered in doctors' offices, hospitals, and rehab facilities. But all that changed in the early 1980s when a stunned public learned that the gifted "girl-next-door"—America's singing sweetheart—had literally starved herself to death. From that day forward, *anorexia* has been a familiar word.

The obvious question both then and now is: *Why would anyone enter into self-starvation*, especially if they, like Karen, "had it all"—fame, family, fortune? In truth, Karen's battle with anorexia began as a desperate and deliberate attempt to eliminate her curves because she loathed her "hourglass figure."[5]

At age 17, the 5' 4" brunette began focusing on her figure when she reached 145 pounds. At that point, she went on a diet, and in six months lost 25 pounds, then maintained an average weight of 120 pounds for the next six years.[6] But in August 1973, Karen was appalled at pictures of herself in a concert. An unflattering dress revealed what Karen perceived to be a bloated belly, and then her painful journey began.[7]

Those in the throes of this debilitating eating disorder continually struggle with a warped sense of beauty and a distorted self-image, and if asked, they would be the first to admit the accuracy of these words from the Bible: *"Charm is deceptive, and beauty is fleeting"* (Proverbs 31:30).

▶ **Anorexia** is an eating disorder characterized by compulsive, chronic self-starvation with a refusal to maintain a body weight within 15% of a person's normal weight.[8] The word "disorder" indicates that the normal function of the mind and/or body is impaired.

▶ **Anorexia** is derived from a Greek word that means "without appetite,"[9] which is actually "a misnomer because loss of appetite is rare."[10] However, after the body goes without nourishment for three days, natural hunger subsides, at least for a period of time.

▶ **Anorexics** weigh far less than what should be their normal body weight, which is different for every person, based on age, height, gender, bone structure, and muscle mass. Body weight that is 15% below normal poses a serious threat to physical health.[11] (Sometimes the word "Manorexia" is used for males.)

▶ **Anorexics** may experience a different cause for this *life-threatening* eating disorder than the irrational fear of weight gain or distorted body image. (For example, if you believed that God told you to eat and drink nothing indefinitely— and that to consume anything would be a clear act of rebellion against His Supreme Deity—then out of obedience you could become anorexic and literally starve yourself to death. Someone like this may be suffering from a type of obsessive-compulsive disorder known as "scrupulosity.")

Regardless of the reason for the lack of eating, the Bible says ...

> "My knees give way from fasting;
> my body is thin and gaunt."
> (Psalm 109:24)

WHAT IS Anorexia Nervosa?

When it came to consuming food, Karen Carpenter displayed willpower—*to a fault.*

Unlike bulimics, who binge on food and then purge it, Karen was never found "raiding the fridge" for favorites like ice cream or keeping hidden candy. Her world revolved around weight *loss*—every potential calorie was a threat. Karen's spiral downward into a full-fledged eating disorder began in November 1973 following an appearance on a Bob Hope TV special.

After viewing the videotape, Karen was distressed by how she looked, and Richard, her brother and singing partner, agreed that she looked heavier than before.

Richard passed off the conversation as insignificant, yet Karen vowed "to do something about it."[12] In the process, she abandoned logical, adult reasoning and embraced irrational, deceptive thoughts, seeing herself through the distorted lenses of her flawed perceptions.

Sadly, she shared the distressing thoughts of the psalmist: *"How long must I wrestle with my thoughts and day after day have sorrow in my heart? How long will my enemy triumph over me?"* (Psalm 13:2).

Being deceived, Karen did not heed the words of God ...

**"Give careful thought to your ways."
(Haggai 1:5)**

Those afflicted with anorexia are assaulted by a barrage of obsessive thoughts about body image and food and are consumed with irrational fear and anxiety.

▶ **Anorexia Nervosa** is an intense fear of gaining weight or becoming fat even though a person is dangerously underweight (at least 15% below normal).[13]

▶ **Anorexia Nervosa** is "psychological" in that the *mind* pictures a distorted image of what the body looks like and produces an abnormal fear of weight gain.[14]

The two subtypes are:[15]

- "Restricting Anorexics" maintain their dangerously low weight by excessively restricting their eating and possibly excessively exercising their bodies.

- "Binge/Purge Anorexics" restrict their eating but also purge by self-induced vomiting and/ or the use of laxatives, diuretics, or enemas. They may also engage in binge eating.

Many anorexics move back and forth between these two subtypes.

Sadly, it's as though they are living out the words from the book of Job ...

> **"Someone may be chastened on a bed of pain with constant distress in their bones, so that their body finds food repulsive and their soul loathes the choicest meal. Their flesh wastes away to nothing, and their bones, once hidden, now stick out."**
> **(Job 33:19–21)**

Body Image

QUESTION: **"What is meant by the term 'body image'?"**

ANSWER: Your body image refers to what you ...

▶ **See** when you look at your reflection in a mirror

▶ **Picture** in your mind when you think of your body

▶ **Believe** about your physical appearance

▶ **Feel** about your body—your features, height, weight, shape, size, hair, and skin color

▶ **Sense** in your body when being physically active (gesturing, talking, walking, running, biking, singing, dancing, playing sports, exercising, etc.)

▶ **Think** about the degree of control you have over your body

▶ **Consider** to be your level of comfort in your body

People generally have either a positive or a negative body image.

A negative body image involves ...

▶ A **distorted** view of your physical body, perceiving parts of your body inaccurately

▶ A **belief** that others are attractive but that you are ugly both inside and outside

▶ A **belief** that your undesirable physical appearance reflects negatively on your character or worth

▶ A **sense** of shame regarding your body, feeling embarrassed and uncomfortable about it

▶ A **feeling** of uneasiness and awkwardness in your body

▶ A **feeling** of necessity to obsess over your body

Having a negative body image sets you up for the likelihood of developing an eating disorder, becoming obsessed with weight loss, and experiencing depression, isolation, and low self-esteem.

A positive body image involves ...

▶ A **realistic** view of your physical body, perceiving the parts of your body accurately

▶ An **attitude** of acceptance and approval toward your body

▶ A **belief** that your physical appearance in no way reflects your character or worth

- An **appreciation** for and contentment with your body

- An **absence** of fixating on food, weight, or calories

- An **inner peace** and feeling at ease in your body

Having a positive body image positions you to have a healthy body, to engage in healthy eating, to enjoy a number of healthy relationships and ultimately, the freedom to be all that God created you to be by His design.

"Do you not know that you are God's temple and that God's Spirit dwells in you?"
(1 Corinthians 3:16 ESV)

WHAT IS Anorexia Athletica?

Many people caught in the cruel web of compulsive weight loss are also caught in the snare of compulsive exercise. The two compulsions work hand in hand for those seeking to control their weight, not only by controlling their caloric intake, but also by controlling the amount of calories their bodies burn up through excessive exercise. They abuse their bodies—through both starvation and severe workouts. These desperate souls create their own horrific experience by starving their bodies while working them to death.

Unlike the Israelites, who worked under the whip of the Egyptians, those who are enslaved to anorexia athletica all too often whip themselves into early graves. Also unlike the Israelites, who cried out to God for a deliverer, these slaves suffer in silence. But God hears their unvoiced cry and yearns to deliver them from their cruel taskmaster just as He delivered the children of Israel.

"The LORD said, 'I have indeed seen the misery of my people in Egypt. I have heard them crying out because of their slave drivers, and I am concerned about their suffering. So I have come down to rescue them from the hand of the Egyptians and to bring them up out of that land into a good and spacious land, a land flowing with milk and honey ... '" (Exodus 3:7–8).

▶ **Anorexia Athletica** is also called "compulsive exercise," "obligatory exercise," "exercise addiction," and "activity disorder" and refers to those who no longer exercise for pure enjoyment, but feel compelled to exercise more and more excessively over time.[16]

▶ **Anorexia Athletica** sufferers live to do physical workouts.

- They experience severe guilt and anxiety after missing a workout, and not even exhaustion, depression, anxiety, sickness, or injury can stop them from fulfilling their perceived need for exercise.[17]

- With excessive stress on the heart, an unhealthy diet, and when damage done to the body is not allowed to heal, the end result can be severe depression and even death.

Although exercise, in and of itself, is not wrong, the Bible presents exercise in its proper perspective.

"Physical training is of some value, but godliness has value for all things, holding promise for both the present life and the life to come." (1 Timothy 4:8)

WHAT IS Bulimia?

In the period of history known as the Greco-Roman era, lifestyles of the opulent included lavish feasts and banquets, unabashed indulgences, and sometimes orgies. One common practice was vomiting after overindulging in food and alcohol. Today the practice of "bingeing and purging" still occurs—a pattern characteristic of bulimia. In comparison to anorexia, bulimia is more frequent, harder to diagnose, more secretive, and often coexists with anorexia.

While the Bible instructs us to purge ourselves of impure evil thoughts and actions, it never suggests that we are to purge ourselves of the food our bodies require for sustenance.

" ... Jesus declared all foods clean." (Mark 7:19)

▶ **Bulimia** comes from a Greek word meaning "great hunger."[18]

- The constant and abnormal appetite of a bulimic is an emotional hunger that no amount of food can fill.

19

- The hunger that bulimics have is not necessarily a physical hunger.

- They binge in an effort to fill their three God-given inner needs for love, significance, and security.

- They then purge to get rid of the guilt from eating too much, as well as to maintain or lose more weight.[19]

▶ **Bulimia** is a psychological eating disorder characterized by repeated or sporadic "binge and purge" episodes. Over time, some bulimics ruminate their food.

- *Bingeing* is an unrestrained consumption of large amounts of food in any setting in a short amount of time.

- *Purging* may be done by the intentional vomiting of food or by the use of laxatives and diuretics.

- *Rumination* is the unforced regurgitation, chewing, and re-swallowing of food like a cow chewing its cud.[20]

The Bible states a clear position on the misuse of "the stomach" ...

"Their destiny is destruction, their god is their stomach, and their glory is in their shame. Their mind is set on earthly things."
(Philippians 3:19)

The compulsion not to eat, indeed proved catastrophic for Karen Carpenter.

In January 1982, Karen began seeing a therapist five times a week for 11 months, which met with problematic, not positive, results. By the end of the year, Karen weighed 80 pounds. She was hospitalized and underwent a medical procedure that increased her weight by 25 pounds, but Richard still felt quite unsettled.[21]

Although her body appeared healthier, Karen's energy had been sapped from the years of physical and emotional struggle. Most disturbing of all, according to Richard, "life had gone out of her eyes."[22] Tragically, about three months later, life had gone out of her body.

Karen's untimely death left many questions unanswered for her family and fans. One question begs to be answered by all who put their lives at risk over food ...

> **"Why do I put myself in jeopardy
> and take my life in my hands?"
> (Job 13:14)**

▶ **Obsessions** are intrusive anxiety-producing thoughts that preoccupy the struggler's mind.

"God says I must fast. If I eat food, I am guilty of disobeying Him. Eating food is bad and sinful."

▶ **Compulsions** are persistent drives or irresistible impulses to behave in ways that tend to become irrational.[23]

"I must fast, walk, and pray, but I must not eat. I will not eat!"

Compulsions drive those with an eating disorder to eliminate food or fat by a variety of means: strict dieting and fasting, emetics and self-induced vomiting, multiple laxatives and diuretics, strenuous physical exercise and smoking, Attention Deficit Disorder medications and diet pills, and drinking large amounts of caffeinated coffee and tea.

- An *emetic* is a drug that causes vomiting.

- A *laxative* is a drug that causes bowel elimination.

- A *diuretic* is a drug that causes an increase in the flow of urine.

The struggler who is controlled by these obsessions and compulsions is severely out of control.

"Like a city whose walls are broken through is a person who lacks self-control."
(Proverbs 25:28)

CHARACTERISTICS

No one is looking. So England's Deputy Prime Minister heads for the can opener.[24]

He holds a can of sweetened condensed milk, but there are no plans to whip up a delicious pastry. Instead, he removes the lid, raises the can to his lips, and revels in the golden, velvety flow streaming into his mouth. Ah, relief—a welcomed distraction from the day's stressful demands as a politician.

But John Leslie Prescott is just getting started. Mouthwatering trifles await his tasting, alongside burgers, biscuits, and beloved fish and chips. He'll also make room for his favorites at the neighborhood Chinese restaurant.

Looking back on his 20 years of binge eating and purging, Prescott recalls: "I ... took refuge in stuffing my face."[25]

Scripture, on the other hand, directs us to take refuge elsewhere ...

"My God is my rock, in whom I take refuge, my shield and the horn of my salvation. He is my stronghold, my refuge and my savior ... "
(2 Samuel 22:3)

Pauline Prescott is woefully aware of the warning signs concerning her husband. Large amounts of food continually disappear, and she shares, "the signs in the toilet gave it away." John Prescott excuses himself at restaurants often to go to the bathroom mid-meal, and then returns to eat as if taking his very first bite of food.

But to diagnose Prescott with an eating disorder can certainly seem perplexing because he simply doesn't "look" the part. When his wife gets him to go to a doctor for bulimia, he sits elbow to elbow in a waiting room with young women, so many who are underweight. Meanwhile, Prescott is male, middle-aged, and unmistakably rotund.

"I found it difficult as a man like me to admit that I suffered from bulimia," he confesses. "I never (initially) admitted to this out of the shame and embarrassment."[26]

It's not unusual for embarrassment to blanket those struggling with bulimia. They feel overwhelming shame knowing they are out of control. And they feel afraid that people will find out about their shame/enslavement. Instead of God being their God, food has become their god. Interestingly, the Bible says, *"Don't you know that when you offer yourselves to someone as obedient slaves, you are slaves to the one you obey—whether you are slaves to sin, which leads to death, or to obedience, which leads to righteousness?"* (Romans 6:16–17).

Binge episodes are often compared to ...

▶ Feeling instantaneously comforted

▶ Experiencing a physical high

▶ Going on autopilot

▶ Losing control

▶ Numbing out

Overcompensatory behaviors are a means of getting rid of excess calories and regaining control over mind, body, and food. In reality, those who engage in such maladaptive behaviors only end up feeling famished and emotionally empty again, which leads to another uncontrollable binge, and the cycle repeats itself. Bulimics engage in extreme obsessive-compulsive eating and exercising (anorexia athletica) habits, which often flow over into other destructive behaviors, such as sexual promiscuity, pathological lying, and shoplifting.

Bulimics ...

▶ Practice a strict diet with intervals of binge eating—consuming large amounts of food in a short period of time

▶ Communicate great guilt or severe shame stemming from eating so much

▶ Cope with emotional stress through overeating/ bingeing

▶ Focus excessively on their body shape and weight while they may be normal or even underweight

They ...

▶ Practice self-induced vomiting after eating

▶ Suffer from general depression

▶ Lack self-control when it comes to food

▶ Experience possible fluctuations in weight

▶ Exercise excessively and compulsively

▶ Base self-worth on personal performance

▶ Abuse laxatives or diuretics

▶ Push their bodies way beyond normal healthy limits

Those who binge and purge cannot be at rest. Their obsession over food allows them no peace. They could have written these words spoken by Job himself ...

> **"I have no peace, no quietness;**
> **I have no rest, but only turmoil."**
> **(Job 3:26)**

Each of John Prescott's eating binges averages about 7,000 calories, a tremendous influx of food that traumatizes the entire body. Although Prescott suffers with shame for years, in 2008 he goes public with his private battle, desiring to help others who struggle with the same shame. He wants to destigmatize bulimia and encourage people not to suffer alone. "I eventually managed to control it and to stop it a few years ago," he says. "I want to say to the millions of people, do take advice, it can help and it can help you out of a lot of misery that you suffer in silence."[27]

The principle of Prescott's efforts to help others is found in Scripture ...

"Carry each other's burdens, and in this way you will fulfill the law of Christ." (Gal. 6:2)

How Bulimia Affects Your Body

▶ **Blood Problems**

- Anemia

- Poor circulation, low body temperature, low blood pressure

- Hypertension (high blood pressure)

- Ketoacidosis (high levels of acid buildup in the blood)

- Type 2 diabetes mellitus

▶ **Body Fluids**

- Dehydration
- Low potassium, magnesium, sodium (Out of balance electrolytes can cause cardiac arrest.)

▶ **Kidneys**

- Problems from diuretic abuse
- Infections from vitamin deficiencies, dehydration, and low blood pressure

▶ **Intestines**

- Abdominal cramping and bloating
- Chronic constipation and diarrhea
- Irregular bowel movements, abnormal bowel function
- Bowel dependance on laxatives due to excessive use, causing bowels to no longer function without laxatives

▶ **Hormones**

- Irregular or absent period
- Imbalances causing multiple problems throughout the body
- Imbalances can occur even after recovery when healthy eating habits are being practiced

▶ **Brain**

- Distorted body image
- Excessive fear of weight gain

- Anxiety and depression
- Dizziness
- Seizures
- Difficulty concentrating
- Low self-esteem and shame
- Neurological and mental deterioration

▶ **Cheeks/Jaw Area**

- Swelling, soreness, temporormandibular joint syndrome (TMJ)
- Swollen salivary glands in cheeks

▶ **Mouth**

- Purging of food, which brings up hydrochloric acid from stomach that washes across the teeth
- Teeth sensitive to hot and cold foods and beverages
- Tooth enamel erosion and discoloration (teeth appear transparent)
- Cavities and tooth loss
- Gum disease and pain
- Sores in the mouth, swollen salivary glands in the cheeks

▶ **Throat and Esophagus**

- Sore and irritated
- Tears and ruptures
- Esophageal reflux, damage to larynx and lungs

- Bleeding esophagus
- Cancer of the esophagus, larynx, and throat

▶ **Muscles**

- Fatigue and aching
- Atrophy

▶ **Stomach**

- Pain and soreness
- Delayed emptying
- Ulcers and ruptures
- Deficiency in digestive enzymes
- Pancreatitis caused by repeated stomach trauma

▶ **Skin**

- Abrasions and calluses on knuckles
- Dry flaky skin

▶ **Heart**

- High cholesterol
- Elevated triglyceride levels
- Electrolyte imbalances
- Irregular heartbeat
- Heart muscle weakened, thickened
- Heart failure (mortality rate from 5% to 15% of bulimics due to cardiac arrest)

▶ **Lungs**

- Shortness of breath

- Increased infections

▶ **Eyes**

- Broken blood vessels, retinal detachment resulting from vomiting

- Vision problems

▶ **Pregnancy and Delivery Problems**

- Miscarriage

- Difficulty getting pregnant

- Baby stillborn (not born alive)

- Baby born early and low birth weight

- Birth defects, such as blindness or mental retardation

▶ **Drastic Weight Fluctuations**

- Chronic bingeing/purging causes extreme weight fluctuation within short periods of time.

Tragically, those who believe the lies that produce and propagate this fatal eating disorder, have failed to guard their hearts and their minds, thereby putting their lives in danger. No wonder Scripture strongly admonishes us to ...

**"Above all else, guard your heart,
for everything you do flows from it."
(Proverbs 4:23)**

They're known as "Thinspiration," famous female celebrities idolized by anorexics and praised on pro-anorexia websites for their skeletal frames.

One of the most popular "Thinspiration" figures is Victoria Beckham, formerly known as Posh Spice of the Spice Girls, a British pop music group with a string of hits in the 1990s. A posting on one website reads, "I envy her thin legs and chest. She has beautiful bones sticking out of her chest."[28]

The glamorization of anorexia is closely linked to a consistent message from all different types of media: You can't be thin enough.

Those who struggle with anorexia are hungry for love—they feel love-starved. Their deepest hunger for love can be satisfied only by the One who *is* love—God Himself.

Realize, people will let you down. People can only provide a temporary filling of love that will once again end in hunger for love. No one has demonstrated more love to you than God has, love that has tremendous potential impact both now and for all eternity.

The Scripture speaks of His continual love for you ...

**"Praise be to God, who has not rejected my prayer or withheld his love from me!"
(Psalm 66:20)**

Those who suffer with anorexia nervosa have a "fat phobia," an intense fear of gaining weight. Their desired weight represents their self-worth, self-control, and status.

They generally fall into the following two subgroups, with many crosses back and forth between the two during the course of their illness.

1. Restricting food intake and possibly exercising excessively (anorexia athletica)

2. Bingeing and purging food

Anorexics …

▶ Deny ever feeling hungry

▶ Postpone major events

▶ Refuse to maintain even minimal body weight

▶ Put their life on hold until they "get thin"

They …

▶ Exercise excessively

▶ Diet exceedingly

▶ Weigh frequently

▶ Commonly experience hair loss

They constantly …

▶ Obsess about food, calories, and nutrition

▶ Feel bloated, fat, or nauseated from eating even small amounts of food

▶ See themselves as fat when they are truly too thin

▶ Believe they are overweight even while continuously losing weight

Additionally, they necessarily ...

▶ Feel cold even when the temperature is normal

▶ Set unobtainable performance goals for themselves

▶ Experience amenorrhea (the absence of menstrual cycles)

▶ Avoid mirrors and photos and engage in constant self-criticism that sabotages self-esteem

For those in the midst of the struggle no matter what they do, their hearts are not at peace. Their pain is ever-present.

They can feel the hurt spoken by Job in his deep suffering ...

> **"If I speak, my pain is not relieved;**
> **and if I refrain, it does not go away."**
> **(Job 16:6)**

In her autobiography, Victoria admits to having an eating disorder and being consumed with her appearance while singing with the Spice Girls. "It was awful," she recollects. "I was very obsessed. I could have told you the calorie and fat content in anything." A picture published in a British newspaper came with the headline "Skeletal Spice."[29]

Many hear the term "eating disorder" and feel little (if any) concern because they have little (if any) knowledge of the meaning of the term. However, others hear "eating disorder" and feel paralyzed with fear—hearts race, palms sweat, minds swirl. Why?

The reason is quite simple. They know all too well this lying, conniving, murdering thief. They've seen its bony fingers choke the life out of a precious loved one while whispering words of deception. They've seen the deadly stranglehold and have felt helpless to lend a hand. Those who have watched a loved one drink its poisonous words have seen an eating disorder destroy a life, a family, even a community. They are far too familiar with the hideous and horrendous ways it can destroy a person's body, mind, and spirit.

They know because they have lived it. They have seen up close and personal the physical complications of anorexia nervosa and its deadly twin, bulimia nervosa.

What they may not know is that humility of heart and reverence for God are key factors in having a healthy body.

"Do not be wise in your own eyes; fear the Lord and shun evil.
This will bring health to your body and nourishment to your bones."
(Proverbs 3:7–8)

How Anorexia Affects Your Body

▶ **Brain and Nerves**

- Cognitive impairment, disordered thinking, extreme forgetfulness, seizures due to malnutrition

- Irrational fear of weight gain

- Sadness, depression

- Moodiness, irritability

- Fainting, dizziness

- Changes in brain chemistry

- Numbness or sensations in hands or feet (neuropathy)

- Structural changes (reduction in gray matter) and abnormal brain activity (sometimes permanent)

▶ **Hair**

- Thinning hair gives a balding appearance.

- Brittle hair falls out, white fuzz (called lanugo) appears on the body to help keep it warm.

▶ Heart

- Reduced blood flow
- Slow heart rate, irregular rhythms
- Abnormally low blood pressure
- Fluttering of the heart (palpitations)
- Decreased size of heart (Muscles shrink from starvation.)
- Electrolyte imbalance
- Heart attack
- Heart failure

▶ Blood

- Anemia
- Low levels of vitamin B12, causing anemia
- Low production of blood cells
- Lack of red blood cells (life-threatening)

▶ Malnutrition

- Brittle nails
- Low body weight
- Respiratory infections
- Blindness
- Death

▶ Psychological Problems

- Distorted view—seeing themselves as fat even though they are "skin and bones"

- Anxiety, depression, suicide

- Insomnia

▶ Reproductive Problems

- Infertility

- Miscarriage

- C-section

- Complicated deliveries

- Baby with low birth weight

- Birth defects

- Postpartum depression

▶ Muscles, Joints, and Bones

- Muscle atrophy (wasting away of muscle and decrease in muscle mass) resulting from the body feeding off of itself

- Weak muscles, swollen joints, temporary paralysis

- Chronic fatigue syndrome related to weakened immune system

- Loss of bone minerals (osteopenia)

- Loss of bone density (osteoporosis), fractures, brittle bones

- Lack of hormones and vitamin deficiencies (arthritis)

- Failure to develop strong bones in children and teenage girls

- Slowed growth in children and adolescents

- Stunted growth in boys due to declining testosterone levels

▶ **Kidneys**

- Kidney stones

- Kidney failure

▶ **Body Fluids**

- Dehydration can lead to kidney failure, seizures, and brain damage.

- Low potassium, magnesium, sodium, and electrolyte imbalance can cause heart failure.

- Hyponatremia (insufficient sodium in the blood) can result from drinking too much water too quickly, causing the lungs to fill with fluid, the brain to swell, vomiting, confusion, and death.

- Edema (swelling of soft tissues) can result from excess water retention.

- Refeeding Syndrome (life-threatening fluid and electrolyte shifts) can result from aggressive nutritional support therapies—nutritional support needs to increase slowly.

▶ Intestines/Gastrointestinal Problems

- Abdominal pain, cramps, and bloating

- Constipation and diarrhea

- Gastric rupture, stomach erosion, or perforation

- Gastrointestinal bleeding, Crohn's Disease

▶ Hormones

- Cessation of menstrual cycle (amenorrhea)—when fat levels drop below 22% of normal weight, deficiency in fat (essential for good health), causing menstrual cycles to stop

- Growth stunted

- Decreased reproductive hormones

- Hypothyroidism (low thyroid levels)

- Higher stress hormone levels

- Hypoglycemia (low blood sugar) causing fatigue, dizziness, headaches

▶ Skin

- Bruise easily

- Dry, yellow skin

- Growth of fine hair all over body (lanugo)

- Low body temperatures

- Brittle nails

- Dark circles under the eyes

▶ **Dental problems**

- Decalcification of teeth

- Erosion of tooth enamel

- Severe staining and decay

- Gum disease (gingivitis, periodontitis)

▶ **Organ Problems**

- Prolonged lack of calories leads to dangerously high blood levels of liver enzymes.

- Multiple organ failure results in death.

- Pancreatitis can result from digestive enzymes related to repeated stomach trauma.

▶ **Drastic Weight Loss**

- The self-starvation of the anorexic causes the body weight to drop so low that kidneys and other organs start to shut down, leading to death.

Make no mistake—anorexia is life-threatening. Therefore, don't be in denial. Like this admission in the Psalms, admit your anguish and weakness—that's the first step toward healing ...

"My life is consumed by anguish and my years by groaning; my strength fails because of my affliction, and my bones grow weak." (Psalm 31:10)

Note: If you are experiencing any of these physical or emotional problems, be sure to consult your health-care professional immediately.

Since the entire body is impacted by the presence of life-sustaining food, the absence of food also impacts the whole body—specifically the brain. This makes it increasingly more difficult for the sufferer to make sound decisions because the mind is not sharp and thinking is murky. They are unable to know the peace of God because their minds are unable to trust completely in God.

The Bible says about Him ...

> **"You [God] will keep in perfect peace those whose minds are steadfast, because they trust in you.
> (Isaiah 26:3)**

A recent study has shown that brain function in those who suffered and recovered from anorexia is different from those who have never suffered from an eating disorder.[30] Some of those differences have included ...

▶ Brain function in recovered anorexic women showed little emotional response to winning or losing a simple game, while brain function in non-anorexic women revealed a stronger emotional response to the same situation.

▶ Brain function in recovered anorexic women showed little difference in distinguishing positive and negative feedback, while brain function in non-anorexic women revealed stronger degrees of activity when discriminating between positive and negative responses.

▶ Brain function in recovered anorexic women showed stronger emphasis on strategic methods of game play, while brain function in non-anorexic women revealed greater enjoyment of game play.

▶ Brain function in recovered anorexic women revealed undue worry over making mistakes and a desire to discover "rules" where none exist, while brain function in non-anorexic women showed an aptitude for making choices and then moving on more easily.

Clearly, anyone who is starving becomes preoccupied with food, just like the anorexic. Interestingly, this food obsession can disappear with normal caloric intake. Just as a well-oiled engine runs silently and smoothly, a well-fed brain is able to take thoughts captive and control unhealthy urges.

> **" ... we take captive every thought
> to make it obedient to Christ."
> (2 Corinthians 10:5)**

CAUSES

Hers should have been a storybook life—complete with the happiest ending—but although she lived in a palace, the princess couldn't hide the pain. Lady Diana Spencer walked the aisle and onto the world stage when she married Prince Charles on July 29, 1981, and became Princess Diana. The 20-year-old bride was beautiful, bashful, and immediately beloved. She would go on to become one of the most famous women in the world, her every move recorded, photographed, adored. But what went on behind closed castle doors didn't fit with the regal, public façade.

Prince Charles' previous longtime romantic relationship with Camilla Parker Bowles interfered with Diana's marriage and resulted in the prince's ensuing adultery. Both Diana's marriage and her spirit were broken. Thus, the princess would seek consolation in food—large amounts of food. Yet it was only a fleeting fix for her pain, for she would always purge it back up.

"Rampant bulimia" was her recourse upon learning that Prince Charles had resumed his relationship with Camilla.[31] Her external out-of-control bingeing and purging merely reflected her internal depth of despair.

"So my heart began to despair over all my toilsome labor under the sun."
(Ecclesiastes 2:20)

Diana described "a feeling of being no good at anything and being useless and hopeless and failed in every direction."[32]

Her husband's love for another woman also led to increased isolation. Diana recalled Charles' friends labeling her sick, unstable, and in need of being put in some sort of home to get better. "I was almost an embarrassment."[33]

The Princess of Wales was a princess in pain. She felt helpless over her husband's infidelity, and she felt inadequate around the Royal Family. "Anything good I ever did nobody ever said a thing, never said, 'well done,'" she shared. "But if I tripped up, which invariably I did, because I was new at the game, a ton of bricks came down on me."[34]

By her own admission, the rejection and loneliness led her into an illicit affair; her low self-worth was the setup for her eating disorder. And because of her husband's betrayal, her dignity was damaged and her security was destroyed.

Any struggler in such emotional pain could identify with the suffering of Job ...

> **"Terrors overwhelm me; my dignity
> is driven away as by the wind,
> my safety vanishes like a cloud."
> (Job 30:15)**

In a 1995 interview, Princess Diana contemplated her marriage into the royal family and the accompanying adjustments with life in the limelight. Diana believed she had Charles' support with her role, but it wouldn't take long for the media to put a strain on their marriage. She, not he, would become the media darling, a source of "phenomenal" pressure while trying to publicly operate as a couple.[35]

Diana's struggles with insecurity surfaced early on, even hinting at the deception and distortion over personal appearance that accompanies bulimia. She in no way saw herself as the world saw her: "As far as I was concerned I was a fat, chubby, 20-year-old, 21-year-old, and I couldn't understand the level of interest."[36]

The eyes of the world were riveted on England as the death of Princess Diana stirred profound interest in the details of her life. Of paramount interest was her struggle with an eating disorder. Reports depicted the princess as having a monumental appetite, yet pictures portrayed a beautiful woman who was "stylishly" thin. Eventually, in public interviews she admitted to the world that she had bouts with bulimia.

Both anorexia and bulimia are addictive behaviors, yet they are part of a syndrome of suffering that is never beyond God's healing hand.

> **"Heal me, LORD, and I will be healed;**
> **save me and I will be saved ... "**
> **(Jeremiah 17:14)**

Denial, the mental process that leads addicts to conclude they are okay and do not have a problem, is common among those suffering with various forms of eating disorders. Defiance is often the result when confronted with the possibility of illness.

If you are concerned about someone struggling with anorexia or bulimia, review the following checklist and mark behaviors you have observed. This could be the first step in planning an intervention if it becomes necessary. Seeing something written, something tangible, might help raise red flags and initiate movement toward the road to recovery. A consultation with a *medical professional* also is highly beneficial.

More often than not, interventions are intense because people with anorexia and bulimia are driven by one solitary fear—the fear of getting fat. Anticipate irrationality and strong emotional displays, but always remember the earlier the intervention, the greater the chance for recovery.[37] Also realize the responsibility you have to do everything within your power to rescue your loved one from the very real and ruthless jaws of death that await all who fail to escape the death grip anorexia and bulimia have on their lives. *"Rescue those being led away to death; hold back those staggering toward slaughter"* (Proverbs 24:11).

Self-Image Checklist

As you read through the following list, check each one that applies to you.

☐ I hate how I look.

☐ I hate how I feel.

☐ I don't like my body.

☐ I feel fat and powerless.

☐ I constantly compare my body to others who are thin.

☐ I would be happy if I could control how I look.

☐ I obsessively weigh myself more than once a day.

☐ I obsessively think about food.

☐ I eat when I'm not hungry.

☐ I eat when I'm stressed, anxious, or bored.

☐ I count calories and fat grams every time I eat.

☐ I hide how many meals I skip.

☐ I hide how much I eat.

☐ I hide how much I vomit.

☐ I hide how much I exercise.

☐ I hide how many laxatives and/or diuretics I take.

☐ I hide my true feelings.

☐ I avoid conflict at all costs.

- ☐ I avoid being around people because I feel fat.

- ☐ I have a hard time eating when other people are present.

- ☐ I have a hard time asking for help.

- ☐ I avoid letting people really know me.

- ☐ I feel a lot of guilt over my past.

- ☐ I feel a sense of shame about who I am.

- ☐ I feel a sense of low self-worth.

- ☐ I feel good because I'm a perfectionist.

- ☐ I wish I could just disappear.

- ☐ I wish I could stop my pain.

If this list accurately reflects your thoughts, feelings, and behaviors, you will quickly and completely identify with the words of Job ...

> " ... I cannot lift my head, for I am full of shame and drowned in my affliction."
> (Job 10:15)

Are You Puzzled over an Eating Disorder?

Puzzles are solved by carefully putting the pieces together to reveal a true picture. When you put the emotional clues together, the picture emerges of a person in pain—one who feels love-starved, security-deprived, or insignificant—one who is caught in a life-threatening cycle.

Learning the truth and living in the truth about the Lord's unfailing love for you are the major pieces needed to begin solving the problem to begin the healing process of becoming whole.

As the nation of Israel did long ago, you also can take great comfort from the Lord's words in Isaiah ...

**"'Though the mountains be shaken
and the hills be removed,
yet my unfailing love for you will not be
shaken nor my covenant of peace be
removed,' says the Lord,
who has compassion on you."
(Isaiah 54:10)**

Princess Diana sought love and attention not from the world, but from those most closely around her.

And yet, they didn't "get it" because she was constantly on the front pages of newspapers and magazines. The last thing she needed, they mistakenly presumed, was more attention.

But the princess continually cried out to the point of injuring herself. "I didn't like myself, I was ashamed because I couldn't cope with the pressures."[38] She would cut herself on her thighs and arms, sometimes even in front of Prince Charles.

An adoring public helped Diana carry through with her official duties and provided some relief from her emotional pain.[39]

Princess Diana described her bulimia as a "secret disease," something you inflict upon yourself because "your self-esteem is at low ebb and you don't think you're worthy or valuable."[40] Stuffing her stomach with food created a false feeling of comfort, like "a pair of arms" around her. But the momentary solace always gave way to disgust as she peered down at her bloated stomach, and Diana would vomit it all up. Not once, not twice, but up to five times a day.[41]

Diana suffered from bulimia for "a number of years," the bingeing and purging occurring daily with alarming frequency during the most stressful periods of her life.[42]

But eating disorders can cover the gamut, with some people engaging in the practice of bingeing and purging only once or twice a week. Others habitually chew their food, savoring the flavor and texture, and then spit it out. And still others will induce vomiting, not after two packages of cookies, but after just two cookies.[43]

Bingeing and purging was an "escape mechanism" for Diana, a distraction from her stress-filled marriage.

**" ... I was overcome by distress and sorrow."
(Psalm 116:3)**

Eating disorders are merely symptoms of the surfacing problems, not the underlying, actual problem. Those suffering from these eating disorders have believed lies and have lost sight of the truth.

But God wants us to face the truth, as seen in this Psalm ...

**"Guide me in your truth and teach me ... "
(Psalm 25:5)**

Those with eating disorders experience ...

▶ **Confusion** over values. What is more important:

- Appearance or achievement?
- Thinness or healthiness?
- Beauty or brains?

▶ **Deception** of self and others

- Pretending to swallow food but spitting it out later

- Cutting food into tiny bites to appear to be eating; secret rituals with food

- Lying about eating

▶ **Depression** over feeling "fat," (although weight is normal or far below—even to the point of looking like "skin and bones")

- Processing information becomes utterly painful.

- Logical thinking becomes virtually impossible.

- Life becomes an unconscious—or a conscious and deliberate—attempt at suicide.

▶ **Compulsion** for some feeling of control

- "Eating is the one part of my life I can control."

- "I can eat as much as I want and still not gain weight."

- "This way I can make the pain go away."

▶ **Loneliness** because of the desire to avoid discovery

- "I just cannot talk to anyone about this problem."

- "I feel claustrophobic if people get too close to me."

- "I long for closeness, yet I'm scared of it."

▶ **Low self-worth** because personal value is based on appearance

  - "I'm a fat pig."

  - "I don't deserve to live."

  - "I don't deserve any help! I am a bad person."

▶ **Perfectionism** because they believe that everything must fit just right, or it's horrible

  - "I must have the perfect body like the models in the magazines."

  - "I must make a perfect appearance or I don't want to appear at all."

  - "I must perform perfectly or no one will love me."

▶ **People pleasing** with an excessive desire for approval

  - "If I'd just done better, my parents wouldn't have divorced."

  - "If I'd just looked better, I wouldn't have been abandoned."

  - "If I'd just weighed less, I might have been loved."

The Bible instead encourages us to evaluate our priorities ...

"For am I now seeking the approval of man, or of God? Or am I trying to please man? If I were still trying to please man, I would not be a servant of Christ." (Galatians 1:10 ESV)

Princess Diana battled bulimia for seven years, and she knew the eating disorders revealed a far deeper problem than "not being able to get into a size 10 dress."[44] While Diana readily admits that societal demands for physical perfection can trigger anorexia or bulimia, there are other causes at work as well, including a distorted relationship with something everyone needs for survival—food.

People with eating disorders "turn nourishment of the body into a painful attack on themselves" and what appears to be a surface environmental cause—vanity—actually goes much deeper.[45]

An eating disorder can become a "shameful friend," according to Diana, because by focusing tremendous energy on controlling the body, a "refuge" has been found for not having to face the more painful issues at hand.[46]

Sadly, those who refuse to face painful truths in their lives most often hate their very lives and reflect the heart of this verse ...

"I loathe my very life; therefore I will give free rein to my complaint and speak out in the bitterness of my soul."
(Job 10:1)

▶ **Feeling worthless** because of abuse in the home

▶ **Feeling inadequate** because of unrealistic expectations of others

- ▶ **Feeling driven** in a high performance atmosphere

- ▶ **Feeling hopeless** as a result of depression from past behaviors

- ▶ **Feeling powerless** because of obesity or other eating disorder in the family

- ▶ **Feeling angry** because of past mistreatment

- ▶ **Feeling anxious** due to stressful life changes

Feelings rather than facts dominate the decisions of those dealing with an eating disorder. The result is increased internal and external chaos because their feelings are skewed, thus they cannot provide a solid basis for making decisions. When distorted feelings rule, desired control is lost because unpredictability reigns, not order. Rather than being in control, feelings need to be controlled. They are designed by God to be the caboose not the engine driving someone's life choices. Reason based on facts is to guide us in making decisions.

"Come now, let us reason together, says the Lord: though your sins are like scarlet, they shall be as white as snow; though they are red like crimson, they shall become like wool. If you are willing and obedient, you shall eat the good of the land; but if you refuse and rebel, you shall be eaten by the sword; for the mouth of the Lord has spoken." (Isaiah 1:18–20 ESV)

Princess Diana believed the root cause of an eating disorder often stems from childhood pain or the self-doubt and uncertainty associated with adolescence.

The pressure of youth who feel the need to be perfect, coupled with their inability "to express their true feelings ... of guilt, of self-revulsion, and low personal esteem" can lead them in adulthood to want to "dissolve like a disprin (aspirin) and disappear," she said, speaking from experience.[47]

By understanding the causes of eating disorders, we can be proactive to help meet the emotional needs of children as a preventative. "As parents, teachers, family and friends, we have an obligation to care for our children. To encourage and guide, to nourish and nurture and to listen with love to their needs, in ways which clearly show our children that we value them. They in their turn will then learn how to value themselves."

Until her untimely death from a car accident in 1997, Princess Diana was a public advocate for the diagnosis and treatment of eating disorders. She put an international spotlight on the troubling issue. Just as Diana longed for children to become adults who "value themselves," a biblical perspective assumes that people recognize their God-given value.

Jesus wants us to recognize and always remember that we are unique creations, masterpieces, and that we are loved beyond measure. He longs for us to realize our value and significance to Him.

If you are suffering from anorexia or bulimia, Jesus can fill the deepest longings of your soul. He loves you with an everlasting love. He has paid for you and claimed you as His very own. He has a perfectly designed plan and purpose for your life. He can provide lasting sustenance for your emotional and spiritual hunger. And He wants you to nourish and take special care of your body because it was compassionately created with the utmost precision. Value yourself, know your God-given worth.

> **"Before I formed you in the womb I knew you, before you were born I set you apart ..." (Jeremiah 1:5)**

Three God-Given Inner Needs

In reality, we have all been created with three God-given inner needs: the needs for love, significance, and security.[48]

▶ **Love**—to know that someone is unconditionally committed to our best interest

"My command is this: Love each other as I have loved you" (John 15:12).

▶ **Significance**—to know that our lives have meaning and purpose

"I cry out to God Most High, to God who fulfills his purpose for me" (Psalm 57:2 ESV).

▶ **Security**—to feel accepted and a sense of belonging

"Whoever fears the Lord has a secure fortress, and for their children it will be a refuge" (Proverbs 14:26).

The Ultimate Need-Meeter

Why did God give us these deep inner needs, knowing that people fail people and self-effort fails us as well?

God gave us these inner needs so that we would come to know Him as our Need-Meeter. Our needs are designed by God to draw us into a deeper dependence on Christ. God did not create any person or position or any amount of power or possessions to meet the deepest needs in our lives. If a person or thing could meet all our needs, we wouldn't need God! The Lord will use circumstances and bring positive people into our lives as an extension of His care and compassion, but ultimately only God can satisfy all the needs of our hearts. The Bible says ...

"The Lord will guide you always;
he will satisfy your needs in a sun-scorched
land and will strengthen your frame.
You will be like a well-watered garden,
like a spring whose waters never fail."
(Isaiah 58:11)

The apostle Paul revealed this truth by first asking, *"What a wretched man I am. Who will rescue me from this body that is subject to death?"* and then by answering his own question in saying it is *"Jesus Christ our Lord!"* (Romans 7:24–25).

All along, the Lord planned to meet our deepest needs for ...

▶ **Love**—*"I [the Lord] have loved you with an everlasting love; I have drawn you with unfailing kindness"* (Jeremiah 31:3).

▶ **Significance**—*"'For I know the plans I have for you,' declares the LORD, 'plans to prosper you and not to harm you, plans to give you hope and a future'"* (Jeremiah 29:11).

▶ **Security**—*"The LORD himself goes before you and will be with you; he will never leave you nor forsake you. Do not be afraid; do not be discouraged"* (Deuteronomy 31:8).

The truth is that our God-given needs for love, significance, and security can be legitimately met in Christ Jesus! Philippians 4:19 makes it plain ...

"My God will meet all your needs according to the riches of his glory in Christ Jesus."

Both the anorexic and the bulimic have an obsessive focus on being thin. The bulimic does not love food any more than the anorexic loves to starve. In fact, the bulimic comes to hate the food just as much as the anorexic does. The bulimic uses food as a means to numb feelings and as a tool to lose weight. It provides something to purge, thereby eliminating calories and leading to weight loss.

▶ WRONG BELIEF

"I'm so fat no one could love me. I hate who I am. The only way I can be loved is to take control of my body and get it to the right size."

"There is a way that appears to be right, but in the end it leads to death" (Proverbs 14:12).

RIGHT BELIEF

"The issue in life is not my size but to see myself through God's eyes. The Lord loves me just as I am. Instead of being consumed by control, I'm choosing to release control of my life and trust the Lord Jesus with every part of my heart."

"Trust in the LORD with all your heart and lean not on your own understanding; in all your ways submit to him, and he will make your paths straight" (Proverbs 3:5–6).

Conclusion—The People's Princess

To the world, Diana appeared healthy, physically, emotionally, a "picture perfect" image that catapulted her to the top of fashion and "most admired" lists. But the hidden truth was that the Princess of Wales was suffering and starving for love.

She often felt misunderstood or ignored by those she needed the most, and the deep hurt manifested itself in desperate acts: " ... you have so much pain inside yourself that you try and hurt yourself on the outside."[49]

Because Diana's weight appeared normal—unlike with anorexics—she believed she could "pretend the whole way through" her seemingly ceaseless bouts of bulimia. But there were those who were watching, whose eyes penetrated through the pretense. Diana would receive comments like, "I suppose you're going to waste that food later on?"[50] Comments like this created additional pressure, prompting her to relieve that pressure the best way she knew—by vomiting.

For bulimics, their tumultuous struggle is something not to be discussed; therefore, Diana never sought help from the Royal Family. "When you have bulimia you're very ashamed of yourself and you hate yourself."[51]

Diana's eventual "going public" about her bulimia gave hope to others. Following Diana's public admission, the number of sufferers who came forward in England doubled, with 60,000 reported cases in the mid 1990s. It was dubbed the "Diana effect," prompting people, primarily young women, to first acknowledge their problem and then to seek treatment.

Anorexia and bulimia may be "secret" problems, but they affect far more people than just the sufferers. During the recovery process, those with eating disorders typically have fits of rage and depression, and their loved ones may have the very strong temptation to pull back emotionally, increasingly withdraw, or "even throw in the towel."

However, the Bible encourages loved ones to ...

> **" ... be patient, bearing with one another in love." (Ephesians 4:2)**

WHAT IS God's Ultimate Plan?

True security is found in relationship with God. Our hearts seek to be bonded, and the one eternal bond is with God, established through a personal relationship with Jesus Christ. That is the ultimate yearning of our soul—to be with God.

"For I am convinced that neither death nor life, neither angels nor demons, neither the present nor the future, nor any powers, neither height nor depth, not anything else in all creation, will be able to separate us from the love of God that is in Christ Jesus our Lord" (Romans 8:38–39).

FOUR POINTS OF GOD'S PLAN

#1 God's Purpose for You is *Salvation*.

What was God's motivation in sending Jesus Christ to earth?

To express His love for you by saving you!

The Bible says, *"God so loved the world that he gave his one and only Son, that whoever believes in him shall not perish but have eternal life. For God did not send his Son into the world to condemn the world, but to save the world through him"* (John 3:16–17).

What was Jesus' purpose in coming to earth?

To forgive your sins, to empower you to have victory over sin, and to enable you to live a fulfilled life!

Jesus said, *"I have come that they may have life, and that they may have it more abundantly"* (John 10:10 NKJV).

#2 Your Problem is *Sin.*

What exactly is sin?

Sin is living independently of God's standard—knowing what is right, but choosing what is wrong.

The Bible says, *"If anyone, then, knows the good they ought to do and doesn't do it, it is sin for them"* (James 4:17).

What is the major consequence of sin?

Spiritual death, eternal separation from God.

Scripture states, *"Your iniquities* [sins] *have separated you from your God"* (Isaiah 59:2).

"The wages of sin is death, but the gift of God is eternal life in Christ Jesus our Lord" (Romans 6:23).

#3 God's Provision for You is the *Savior.*

Can anything remove the penalty for sin?

Yes! Jesus died on the cross to personally pay the penalty for your sins.

The Bible says, *"God demonstrates his own love for us in this: While we were still sinners, Christ died for us"* (Romans 5:8).

What is the solution to being separated from God?

Belief in (entrusting your life to) Jesus Christ as the only way to God the Father.

Jesus says, *"I am the way and the truth and the life. No one comes to the Father except through me"* (John 14:6).

"Believe in the Lord Jesus, and you will be saved ... " (Acts 16:31).

#4 Your Part is *Surrender.*

Give Christ control of your life, entrusting yourself to Him.

"Jesus said to his disciples, 'Whoever wants to be my disciple, must deny themselves and take up their cross [die to their own self-rule] *and follow me. For whoever wants to save their life will lose it, but whoever loses their life for me will find it. What good will it be for someone to gain the whole world, yet forfeit their soul?'"* (Matthew 16:24–26).

Place your faith in (rely on) Jesus Christ as your personal Lord and Savior and reject your "good works" as a means of earning God's approval.

"It is by grace you have been saved, through faith—and this is not from yourselves, it is the gift of God—not by works, so that no one can boast" (Ephesians 2:8–9).

The moment you choose to receive Jesus as your Lord and Savior—entrusting your life to Him—He comes to live inside you. Then He gives you His power to live the fulfilled life God has planned for you.

If you want to be fully forgiven by God and become the person God created you to be, you can tell Him in a simple, heartfelt prayer like this:

PRAYER OF SALVATION

*"God, I want a real relationship with You.
I admit that many times I've chosen to go
my own way instead of Your way.
Please forgive me for my sins.
Jesus, thank You for dying on the cross to
pay the penalty for my sins.
Come into my life to be
my Lord and my Savior.
Change me from the inside out
and make me the person
You created me to be.
In Your holy name I pray. Amen."*

WHAT CAN YOU NOW EXPECT?

If you sincerely prayed this prayer, look what God says about you!

"If the Son sets you free,
you will be free indeed."
(John 8:36)

STEPS TO SOLUTION

Every person who is starved for love needs to truly know and accept the love of the Lord in order to meet this deepest inner need for love.

Our God of love says ...

"I have loved you with an everlasting love;
I have drawn you with unfailing kindness."
(Jeremiah 31:3)

Those who know what it is like to struggle for years with an addiction, or any kind of affliction, know through personal experience the necessity of having faith in God our Savior, who offers hope. He offers true hope—not only for the future but also for the present—through a life-changing relationship with the Lord, who goes before you and will be with you, who will never leave you, nor forsake you.

KEY VERSE TO MEMORIZE

"The Lord himself goes before you
and will be with you;
he will never leave you nor forsake you.
Do not be afraid; do not be discouraged."
(Deuteronomy 31:8)

Key Passage to Read

Do you know that God designed you as a one-of-a-kind creation? Do you know that God considers you so special that He has a personalized plan for your life? Do you realize He knit your body together while you were still inside your mother's womb?

Realize the thoroughness of God's knowledge of you—He states that you are "*wonderfully made.*" Just knowing that His thoughts are always with you will give you comfort for you are always on His mind.

Read Psalm 139 and read out loud the truths from these verses. Then you will begin to see how precious you are to God.

PSALM 139:1–18, 23–24

▶ **God knows** me. v. 1

▶ **God knows** my sitting and rising. v. 2

▶ **God knows** my thoughts. v. 2

▶ **God knows** my going out. v. 3

▶ **God knows** my lying down. v. 3

▶ **God knows** my every way. v. 3

▶ **God knows** my words before I speak. v. 4

▶ **God hems** me in. (He protects me.) v. 5

▶ **God's presence** is behind me and before me. v. 5

▶ **God's hand** is upon me. v. 5

▶ **God's presence** is around me. vv. 5–6

▶ **God's Spirit** is everywhere with me. v. 7

▶ **God cannot** be escaped. v. 7

▶ **God is** in the heavens. v. 8

▶ **God is** in the depths. v. 8

▶ **God is** on the wings of the dawn. v. 9

▶ **God is** on the far side of the sea. v. 9

▶ **God will guide** me where I go. v 10

▶ **God will hold** me tightly. v. 10

▶ **God sees** me as clearly in the dark as in bright sunlight. vv. 11–12

▶ **God created** me. v. 13

▶ **God knit** me together in my mother's womb. v. 13

▶ **God made** me in an awesome way. v. 14

▶ **God created** me in a way that causes wonder. v. 14

▶ **God saw** my frame when I was hidden in my mother's womb. v. 15

▶ **God saw** my unformed body. v. 16

▶ **God ordained** all my days and recorded them in His book. v. 16

▶ **God thinks** of me. v. 17

▶ **God's thoughts** about me are precious. v. 17

▶ **God's thoughts** about me are vast in number. v. 17

▶ **God's thoughts** about me outnumber the grains of sand. v. 18

▶ **God searches** and tests me. v. 23

▶ **God searches** and knows my heart. v. 23

▶ **God tests** me and knows my anxious thoughts. v. 23

▶ **God sees** and leads me. v. 24

▶ **God sees** every offensive way in me. v. 24

▶ **God will** lead me to experience everlasting life. v. 24

People suffering with anorexia or bulimia need to be told *it's not about the food*. They *need* to acknowledge that their true need is to have emotional wounds healed, and they *need* to understand that the starving and the bingeing and purging are actually used as distractions to avoid facing painful feelings in order to circumvent excruciating events.

Anorexics and bulimics also *need* to be firmly told that society's bombarding message that "thinness is the way to happiness" is a lie. People with eating disorders tend to isolate themselves from friends and social activities and experience self-loathing rather than self-acceptance. Healthy eating leads to heightened energy and a more robust attitude toward life.[52]

The primary need of the person suffering with anorexia or bulimia is not the food they need to receive but the Lord they need to believe. They need to know experientially the One who made them and loves them and longs to heal them and meet their deepest inner needs.

"My God will meet all your needs according to the riches of his glory in Christ Jesus." (Philippians 4:19)

If you have concerns or if others have expressed concern about your weight or your eating and exercise patterns, take to heart these general principles.

1. **Agree** to get a thorough medical checkup. This condition is life-threatening!

2. **Acquire** as much knowledge about eating disorders as possible—for yourself and for those close to you.

3. **Attend** weekly (or regular) sessions with a knowledgeable, professional, Christian counselor.

4. **Admit** your inability to control your eating pattern.

5. **Abandon** the idea that you just need more willpower. This is not a diet or willpower problem, but a battle to address strongholds.

6. **Allow** yourself to forgive those who have hurt you and even to forgive yourself.

7. **Act** in total faith on God's power to rescue you.

No single approach to breaking addictions is ever enough because bondage is multi-faceted and must incorporate numerous approaches. All addictions involve not only the body but the heart and soul of those they hold captive.

That being the case, it is understandable that the Bible instructs us to ...

> **"Love the LORD your God with
> all your heart and with all your soul
> and with all your strength."
> (Deuteronomy 6:5)**

Having the grace of God operating in our lives, we are both equipped and empowered to make good use of the following treatment approaches to gain inner healing and to overcome eating disorders.

▶ Care from a medical professional

Anorexia and bulimia exacts a tremendous toll on the body. Health consequences can remain years after harmful eating habits have been conquered. A doctor and dietician can often offer helpful advice and treatment for those who have suffered from an eating disorder.

▶ Counsel from a mental health professional

Deeper issues and insecurities that contribute to an eating disorder must be confronted for lasting change to occur. Often a professional counselor can help direct someone with destructive eating patterns to a healthier view of one's self and of food.

▶ Connection with a community of believers

Being a part of a group who desire to follow Christ, revealing vulnerabilities, and being available to offer and receive support are essential for permanent life change in a believer. Become an active part of a group of Christians to receive spiritual direction and create bonds that can support you when you need it most.

> **"Carry each other's burdens,**
> **and in this way you will fulfill**
> **the law of Christ."**
> **(Galatians 6:2)**

Based on the Bible, your true worth isn't based on your outward appearance but on who you are in Christ. In Him, you are infinitely loved and valued.

**"Neither height nor depth,
nor anything else in all creation,
will be able to separate us from the love of
God that is in Christ Jesus our Lord."
(Romans 8:39)**

According to the Bible, you can know that ...

▶ **You've come into a personal relationship with the Lord Jesus; your true identity is in Christ Himself.**

- You are a new creation in Christ. You are no longer what you were.

- If you allow Jesus to become the focus of your life—not food, not compulsion, but Christ— you will increasingly find freedom.

"Therefore, if anyone is in Christ, the new creation has come: The old has gone, the new is here!" (2 Corinthians 5:17).

▶ **The old "you" died.**

- When you trusted in Christ alone as your Savior, the old "you" died, and He gave you a new nature, a new life, a new identity—in Him.

- Your thinking and behavior patterns may still be compulsive about craving food and obsessive about thinness. These patterns, however, no longer need to control you because Christ has broken the power of your sin.

- As you learn to renew your mind with His truth, He will continue to break those compulsive patterns and set you free.

"I have been crucified with Christ, and I no longer live, but Christ lives in me. The life I now live in the body, I live by faith in the Son of God, who loved me and gave himself for me" (Galatians 2:20).

▶ **Even in the midst of your trials, you are totally accepted by the Father.**

- Regardless of how you've been treated by significant family members and friends, you are given unconditional love and unconditional acceptance from your heavenly Father.

- He loves you just the way you are, but *because* He loves you, *He will change you.* He will take your hand, as a father takes the hand of a little child, and will walk you into freedom.

"'Do not fear, for I have redeemed you; I have summoned you by name; you are mine' (Isaiah 43:1).

"You make your saving help my shield, and your right hand sustains me; your help has made me great" (Psalm 18:35).

▶ **The Spirit of Christ will bring about His control in you.**

- It's not your self-control; it's yielding to the Spirit's *control* in you that will produce positive change. When you are rooted in Christ, He will naturally produce the fruit of self-control in you.

"The fruit of the Spirit is love, joy, peace, forbearance, kindness, goodness, faithfulness, gentleness and self-control. Against such things there is no law" (Galatians 5:22–23).

▶ **Your freedom comes through Christ.**

- Family and friends will be used by God, but total freedom from bondage comes only *through Christ.*

"Because through Christ Jesus the law of the Spirit who gives life has set you free from the law of sin and death" (Romans 8:2).

What Lies Have You Been Told?

▶ **The world** tells you a lie. "You can't be too thin—thin is in!"

▶ **The flesh** tells you to live a lie. "You've got to be thin to be accepted."

▶ **The father of lies**, Satan, tells you *"You will not surely die"* (Genesis 3:4 NKJV).

But Know the Truth

▶ The Truth, Jesus, tells you " ... *the truth will set you free*" (John 8:32).

▶ Be free from being controlled by the opinion of others.

▶ You are free to be the healthy size God created you to be.

▶ The world's super models and movie stars are generally underweight and unhealthy.

**"So if the Son sets you free,
you will be free indeed."
(John 8:36)**

People with eating disorders are love-starved and don't feel valuable. For them, love is spelled T-I-M-E. Express your love by keeping eye contact with them and by spending time with them—a lot of time.

You will show that they do have value if you tangibly reach out to them. Even if they don't seem to respond, they desperately seek your acceptance. They desperately long for unconditional love—the Lord's love.

**"Come to me, all you who are weary and burdened, and I will give you rest. Take my yoke upon you and learn from me, for I am gentle and humble in heart, and you will find rest for your souls."
(Matthew 11:28–29)**

Freedom can be found by anyone in any kind of bondage, but it means facing the facts, assuming responsibility, making choices, taking action, sticking it out.

Finding freedom and living in it takes work, but freedom is worth the labor. Freedom cuts the cords of perfectionism so that your soul can soar to be all that God created you to be.

It was for this purpose that Jesus was sent ...

> "... to bind up the brokenhearted,
> to proclaim freedom for the captives
> and release from darkness for the prisoners
> ... to comfort all who mourn,
> and provide for those who grieve ...
> to bestow on them a crown of beauty
> instead of ashes,
> the oil of joy instead of mourning,
> and a garment of praise
> instead of a spirit of despair."
> (Isaiah 61:1–3)

The Way to Freedom

Your first steps to freedom

▶ **Recognize** that you have an eating disorder.

- Face the truth of your unhealthy weight loss and obsession with fat and food.

- Accept the fact that your life and health are seriously compromised.

▶ **Acknowledge** your need.

- Admit your enslavement to an eating disorder and its power in your life.

- Share your struggle with a trusted friend and break the power of the secret.

▶ **Get** professional help.

- Seek out a therapist experienced in successfully treating those snared by an eating disorder.

- Realize that it is vital to get help in understanding your illness and overcoming its hold on you.

▶ **Discover** your past predispositions.

- Explore the family dynamics that possibly "set you up" to have an eating disorder.

- Evaluate past events that still impact your life today and influence your decision making.

▶ **Identify** your present stressors.

- Examine your life (activities and relationships) and pinpoint areas of stress.

- Reflect on any similarities between past life experiences and present-day situations.

▶ **Avoid** your destructive patterns.

- Recognize activities where food is the focus and break those patterns.

- Replace energy-draining behaviors involving food with enjoyable energy-producing activities that do not involve food.

▶ **Flee** your enticing triggers.

- Reflect on times and events that have entrenched you further in destructive eating behaviors.

- Devise a plan of action to overcome unexpected temptations to skip a meal or to binge/purge.

▶ **Resist** your compelling urges.

- Commit to distract yourself whenever you suddenly feel compelled to "act out" with food.

- Plan an activity you will do when you feel the urge to binge or purge.

You cannot hope to walk in freedom unless you walk in the truth. Tell yourself the truth—"Lord, You created my body—You know what is best for my body." Then pray everyday ...

> **"Teach me your way, O LORD;**
> **that I may walk in your truth;**
> **unite my heart to fear [honor] your name."**
> **(Psalm 86:11 ESV)**

The Way to Sustained Freedom

The way to true and total freedom

▶ **Yield** yourself to God.

- Surrender your life, your heart, your mind, your will, and your emotions to Christ.

- Submit to God's rule in your life over your relationships, your thoughts, and your actions.

"Submit yourselves, then, to God. Resist the devil, and he will flee from you" (James 4:7).

▶ **Claim** your victory in Christ.

- Accept by faith the fact that Christ has set you free from the power of sin and death.

- Act on your faith by thinking, talking, and acting in ways that reflect your position as an overcomer through Christ, as one who has moved from death to life.

"Do not offer any part of yourself to sin as an instrument of wickedness, but rather offer yourselves to God as those who have been brought from death to life; and offer every part of yourself to him as an instrument of righteousness" (Romans 6:13).

▶ **Picture** your success.

- Count yourself dead to the call of temptation that would cause you to give in to sin.

- Consider yourself a citizen of heaven, having submitted to Jesus Christ and walking in total victory over all worldly and fleshly desires.

"Our citizenship is in heaven. And we eagerly await a Savior from there, the Lord Jesus Christ, who, by the power that enables him to bring everything under his control, will transform our lowly bodies so that they will be like his glorious body" (Philippians 3:20–21).

▶ **Replace** lies with truth.

- Reject negative thoughts about yourself and replace them with Scriptures that affirm your value and worth to God and the extent of His commitment to you as His child, His priceless possession.

- Remember that feelings change and cannot be trusted, but God does not change. He is totally trustworthy, and His promises are utterly reliable in every circumstance and at all times.

"Now it is God who makes both us and you stand firm in Christ. He anointed us, set his seal of ownership on us, and put his Spirit in our hearts as a deposit, guaranteeing what is to come. ... since we have these promises, dear friends, let us purify ourselves from everything that contaminates body and spirit, perfecting holiness out of reverence for God" (2 Corinthians 1:21–22; 7:1).

▶ **Devise** a plan for daily success.

- Begin and end each day in prayer, praise, and worship, thanking God and seeking His continued guidance.

- Be sure to lay out a detailed plan for each day that contains your daily activities, including balanced meals, Bible study, Scripture memorization, and other healthy activities.

"As long as he sought the LORD, God gave him success" (2 Chronicles 26:5).

▶ **Enlist** the support of others.

- Get involved in a group Bible study or prayer group where you can study God's Word and share prayer requests with other Christians on a regular basis.

- Gather some accountability friends who will check with you on a daily basis, ask you piercing agreed-upon questions, and pray for you to keep walking in freedom.

"Two are better than one. ... If either of them falls down, one can help the other up. But pity anyone who falls and has no one to help them up" (Ecclesiastes 4:9–10).

"Perfume and incense bring joy to the heart, and the pleasantness of a friend springs from their heartfelt advice" (Proverbs 27:9).

▶ **Throw** away your scales.

- Make it your goal to eat healthy, not to lose or gain weight. Trust God to fulfill His promise to provide for your needs as you delight in Him and focus on His desires for you.

- Manage your life well, maintain a good balance in all areas, make a plan, and then carry out your plan. Lose your scales or they will hold you captive to human traditions.

"See to it that no one takes you captive through hollow and deceptive philosophy, which depends on human tradition and the elemental spiritual forces of this world rather than on Christ" (Colossians 2:8).

▶ **Journal** your journey.

- Realize that it is important for you to remember your journey with Christ into the freedom He died to secure for you.

- Record in a daily journal the ways the Lord is manifesting His power in your life through His mighty acts of deliverance in various areas of your life. Then share them with your loved ones—both young and old—to encourage them and to bring glory to God.

"Fix these words of mine in your hearts and minds; tie them as symbols on your hands and bind them on your foreheads. Teach them to your children, talking about them when you sit at home and when you walk along the road, when you lie down and when you get up. Write them on the doorframes of your houses and on your gates" (Deuteronomy 11:18–20).

Remember this biblical truth as you walk the road of freedom in Christ Jesus ...

"It is for freedom that Christ has set us free. Stand firm, then, and do not let yourselves be burdened again by a yoke of slavery." (Galatians 5:1)

If a little is good, a lot is better, so goes the thinking of overeaters who struggle to find balance in their life—and balance in their diet. Much of the time, when a little is good, *a lot is not!* And at other times, especially for anorexic and bulimic strugglers—if little is good, *less is* not!

In our quest for the best, we can throw out the good and end with the worst. We forget that when God saw all He had created He said, "It is good."

"Healthy" is good. "Balance" is good. Healthy, balanced eating is good, and it is possible—even for the anorexic and bulimic. The questions are: Will you do it? How will you do it? When will you do it? Where will you do it? And what are the ramifications of not doing it?

> **"God saw all that he had made,**
> **and it was very good."**
> **(Genesis 1:31)**

▶ **Decide** to try healthy, balanced eating.

- **Keep** unhealthy foods out of sight and in hard to reach places. Or better yet, don't even buy them.

- **Learn** how to eat healthy, not how to avoid eating or how to purge after eating.

- **Plan** nutritional meals and snacks for each day, sing a variety of foods. Track your calorie intake.

- **Make** a shopping list. Don't shop when you are hungry.

- **Realize** strict diets lead to sure failure. Healthy eating leads to sure success.

- **Reward** yourself for eating healthy, but not with food.

- **Rid** your residence of binge and trigger (usually sugary or starchy) foods. Stock up on healthy snacks.

- **Stop** focusing on weight loss. Focus on healthy, balanced eating.

- **Think** about how a particular food makes your body feel to help determine if it's okay to eat.

▶ **Practice** following these guidelines.

- **Eat three small meals** a day at scheduled times.

- **Eat small snacks** between meals at planned times.

- **Eat meals and snacks** at the dining or breakfast table and never in a vehicle, bedroom, bathroom, or when in a hurry.

- **Eat nothing before or during** meal/snack preparation or after the meal/snack is over.

- **Determine** to truly experience your food noting its color, size, shape, texture, and smell.

- **Eat slowly**, chewing each bite, enjoying the flavor and putting your eating utensil down between bites.

- **Stop** eating and relax several times throughout a meal. Think about anything other than eating, visit with someone, look around the room or out the window.

- **Take** just one or two bites of fattening foods. That small amount won't make a difference to your body.

- **Remind** yourself that everyone feels full and clothes feel tighter around the waist after eating. These feelings will go away as your body digests the food and puts it to use.

As you seek to gain God's perspective on food and strive to make God-honoring decisions regarding your food intake, realize what the Bible says ...

**"So I commend the enjoyment of life,
because there is nothing better
for a person under the sun
than to eat and drink and be glad.
Then joy will accompany them in their toil
all the days of the life God has given them
under the sun."
(Ecclesiastes 8:15)**

While you may not think you have the strength to make the changes, you do as you call on the Lord for strength and perseverance. Let the prayer of your heart echo the promising heart cries found in God's Word. Remember, you are His child and He longs to answer your prayers for healing as you surrender to His loving will.

THE PRAYER OF MY HEART - PSALM 31

"O LORD, I have come to you for protection; don't let me be disgraced. Save me, for you do what is right."

I am Your child—heal me, O Lord. I give myself to You.

"Turn your ear to listen to me; rescue me quickly. Be my rock of protection, a fortress where I will be safe."

I am Your child—heal me, O Lord. I give my heart to You.

"You are my rock and my fortress. For the honor of your name, lead me out of this danger."

I am Your child—heal me, O Lord. I give my will to You.

"Pull me from the trap my enemies set for me, for I find protection in you alone."

I am Your child—heal me, O Lord. I give my soul to You.

*"I will be glad and rejoice in your unfailing love,
for you have seen my troubles, and you care
about the anguish of my soul."*

**I am Your child—heal me, O Lord. I give my
life to You.**

*"Have mercy on me, LORD, for I am in distress.
Tears blur my eyes. My body and soul are
withering away. ... I am wasting away from
within."*

**I am Your child—heal me, O Lord. I give my
all to You.**

*"I am trusting you, O LORD, saying, 'You are my
God!'"*

I am Your child—heal me, O Lord.

(Psalm 31:1–4, 7, 9, 10, 14 NLT)

*Those who struggle with eating
disorders feel they have no control.
They conclude:
Food is the only thing I can control,
how much or how little I consume.
But their deepest need
is not getting control.
It is giving control to Christ.
He is the One who sets them free.*

—JUNE HUNT

SCRIPTURES TO MEMORIZE

Why would people with an eating disorder **despise themselves**?

> *"Those who disregard discipline **despise themselves**, but the one who heeds correction gains understanding."* (Proverbs 15:32)

I've hidden food and my fixation with food so that people know nothing about it. Is it possible to keep my unhealthy eating habits **hidden from God's sight**?

> *"Nothing in all creation is **hidden from God's sight**. Everything is uncovered and laid bare before the eyes of him to whom we must give account."* (Hebrews 4:13)

Why do I feel like my **appetite works** against me and my **hunger drives** me?

> *"The **appetite** of laborers **works** for them; their **hunger drives** them on."* (Proverbs 16:26)

Is it to my benefit **to heed instruction** even when I don't feel like it?

> *"Whoever gives **heed to instruction** prospers, and blessed is the one who trusts in the LORD."* (Proverbs 16:20)

What should be my purpose when I **eat or drink or whatever** I choose to **do**?

> *"Whether you **eat or drink or whatever** you **do**, do it all for the glory of God."* (1 Cor. 10:31)

Don't I have the right to do whatever I want with my **body**—it's my **own**?

> "Do you not know that **your body** is the temple of the Holy Spirit who is in you, whom you have from God, and you are not your **own**." (1 Corinthians 6:19 NKJV)

Can anything I put **into** my **mouth defile** my body?

> "What goes **into** someone's **mouth** does not **defile** them, but what comes out of their mouth, that is what defiles them." (Matthew 15:11)

If **God created everything good**, why do I feel so bad when I eat certain foods?

> "**Everything God created** is **good**, and nothing is to be rejected if it is received with thanksgiving." (1 Timothy 4:4)

If my **enemy is hungry** or **thirsty**, is it wrong to help him?

> "If your **enemy is hungry**, feed him; if he is **thirsty**, give him something to drink." (Romans 12:20)

How can I know that the **heavenly Father** cares about my needs? Am I **valuable** to Him?

> "Look at the birds of the air; they do not sow or reap or store away in barns, and yet your **heavenly Father** feeds them. Are you not much more **valuable** than they?" (Matthew 6:26)

NOTES

1. June Hunt, *The Answer To Anger: Practical Steps to Temper Fiery Emotions* (Eugene: Harvest House, 2009), 11–13.

2. Anonymous, "Dying to be Thin: A Pro-Ana Blog," January 4, 2009, http://anaregzig.blogspot.com/.

3. Anonymous, "Dying to be Thin: A Pro-Ana Blog," http://anaregzig.blogspot.com/.

4. Richard Carpenter, "Introducing Carpenters," http://www.richardandkarencarpenter.com/biography.htm.

5. Richard Carpenter, "At a Cost," http://www.richardandkarencarpenter.com/biography-8.htm.

6. Carpenter, "Enter Karen, The Singer," http://www.richardandkarencarpenter.com/biography-3.htm.

7. Carpenter, "At a Cost"

8. American Psychiatric Association, *Diagnostic and Statistical Manual of Mental Disorders: DSM-IV-TR*, 4th ed. (Washington, DC: American Psychiatric Association, 2002), 583–584.

9. *New Oxford Dictionary of English*, electronic ed. (n.p.: Oxford University Press, 1998).

10. American Psychiatric Association, *DSM-IV-TR*, 583.

11. American Psychiatric Association, *DSM-IV-TR*, 583–584.

12. Carpenter, "At a Cost"

13. American Psychiatric Association, *DSM-IV-TR*, 583.

14. American Psychiatric Association, *DSM-IV-TR*, 583.

15. American Psychiatric Association, *DSM-IV-TR*, 585.

16. Eating DisordersOnline.com, "Anorexia Athletica," http://www.eatingdisordersonline.com/explain/anorathletica.php.

17. Eating DisordersOnline.com, "Anorexia Athletica"

18. *Merriam-Webster's Collegiate Dictionary*, electronic ed. (n.p.: Merriam-Webster, 2001).

19. Minirth, Meier, Hemfelt, Sneed, and Hawkins, *Love Hunger*, (Nashville: Thomas Nelson, 2004) 13.

20. Mayo clinic, "Rumination Syndrome" (Rochester, MN: Mayo Foundation for Medical Education and Research, 2010), http://www.mayoclinic.org/rumination-syndrome/.

21. Carpenter, "Last Performance, Continued Success," http://www.richardandkarencarpenter.com/biography-10.htm.

22. Carpenter, "Last Performance, Continued Success"

23. *The New Shorter Oxford Dictionary of English* (Oxford: Clarendon Press, 1993), s.v. "Compulsion."

24. Sam Jones, "I Took Refuge in Stuffing My Face ... John Prescott Admits Bulimia" *The Guardian*, April 20, 2008, http://www.guardian.co.uk/society/2008/apr/21/health.johnprescott.

25. Jones, "I Took Refuge in Stuffing My Face ... John Prescott Admits Bulimia," http://www.guardian.co.uk/society/2008/apr/21/health.johnprescott.

26. Jones, "I Took Refuge in Stuffing My Face"

27. Jones, "I Took Refuge in Stuffing My Face"

28. Nicole Lampert, "Anorexics Find Posh a Thinspiration," Daily Mail, June 28, 2006.

29. Lampert, "Anorexics Find Posh a Thinspiration"

30. Angela Wagner, Howard Aizenstein, Vijay K. Venkatraman, Julie Fudge, J. Christopher Bay, Laura Mazurkewicz, Guido K. Frank, Ursula F. Bailey, Lorie Fischer, Van Nguyen, Cameron Carter, Karen Putnam, Walter H. Kaye, "Altered Reward Processing in Women Recovered From Anorexia Nervosa" American Journal of Psychiatry, 164 (12) (Arlington, VA: American Psychiatric Association, 2007), 1842, 1849.

31. Martin Bashir, "Diana's 1995 BBC interview," Frontline Online (Boston: WGBH Educational Foundation, 1997), http://www.pbs.org/wgbh/pages/frontline/shows/royals/interviews/bbc.html.

32. Bashir, "Diana's 1995 BBC interview."

33. Bashir, "Diana's 1995 BBC interview."

34. Bashir, "Diana's 1995 BBC interview"

35. Bashir, "Diana's 1995 BBC interview."

36. Bashir, "Diana's 1995 BBC interview."

37. Lynn Ponton, "Coping with Denial in Eating Disorders," (Newburyport, MA: Psych Central, 2006), http://psychcentral.com/lib/2006/coping-with-denial-in-eating-disorders/.

38. Bashir, "Diana's 1995 BBC interview."

39. Bashir, "Diana's 1995 BBC interview."

40. Bashir, "Diana's 1995 BBC interview."

41. Bashir, "Diana's 1995 BBC interview."

42. Bashir, "Diana's 1995 BBC interview."

43. American Psychiatric Association, *DSM-IV-TR*, 594.

44. Diana, Princess of Wales, "Speech on Eating Disorders" (April, 27, 1993), http://www.settelen.com/diana_eating_disorders.htm.

45. Diana, "Speech on Eating Disorders"

46. Diana, "Speech on Eating Disorders"

47. Diana, "Speech on Eating Disorders"

48. Lawrence J. Crabb, Jr., *Understanding People: Deep Longings for Relationship*, Ministry Resources Library (Grand Rapids: Zondervan, 1987), 15–16; Robert S. McGee, *The Search for Significance*, 2nd ed. (Houston, TX: Rapha, 1990), 27–30.

49. Bashir, "Diana's 1995 BBC interview"

50. Bashir, "Diana's 1995 BBC interview"

51. Bashir, "Diana's 1995 BBC interview"

52. Raymond Lemberg, ed. with Leigh Cohn, *Eating Disorders: A Reference Sourcebook*, (Phoenix: Oryx Press, 1999), 166.

June Hunt's HOPE FOR THE HEART minibooks are biblically-based, and full of practical advice that is relevant, spiritually-fulfilling and wholesome.

HOPE FOR THE HEART TITLES

Adultery .... ISBN 9781596366848
Alcohol & Drug Abuse .... ISBN 9781596366596
Anger .... ISBN 9781596366411
Anorexia & Bulimia .... ISBN 9781596369313
Bullying .... ISBN 9781596369269
Codependency .... ISBN 9781596366510
Conflict Resolution .... ISBN 9781596366473
Confrontation .... ISBN 9781596366886
Considering Marriage .... ISBN 9781596366763
Decision Making .... ISBN 9781596366534
Depression .... ISBN 9781596366497
Domestic Violence .... ISBN 9781596366824
Dysfunctional Family .... ISBN 9781596369368
Fear .... ISBN 9781596366701
Financial Freedom .... ISBN 9781596369412
Forgiveness .... ISBN 9781596366435
Friendship .... ISBN 9781596368828
Gambling .... ISBN 9781596366862
Grief .... ISBN 9781596366572
Guilt .... ISBN 9781596366961
Hope .... ISBN 9781596366558
Loneliness .... ISBN 9781596366909
Manipulation .... ISBN 9781596366749
Marriage .... ISBN 9781596368941
Overeating .... ISBN 9781596369467
Parenting .... ISBN 9781596366725
Perfectionism .... ISBN 9781596369214
Reconciliation .... ISBN 9781596368897
Rejection .... ISBN 9781596366787
Self-Worth .... ISBN 9781596366688
Sexual Integrity .... ISBN 9781596366947
Singleness .... ISBN 9781596368774
Stress .... ISBN 9781596368996
Success Through Failure .... ISBN 9781596366923
Suicide Prevention .... ISBN 9781596366800
Verbal & Emotional Abuse .... ISBN 9781596366459

www.aspirepress.com